Willie Macpherson

The Elgin Fiddler

the man   the music   the fiddle

Richard Bennett   Author
Graeme Nairn   Designer

2006

Published by Fraser Macpherson,
Blossom Cottage, Thaxted Road, Wimbish, Essex, CB10 2UZ

© Richard Bennett, Fraser Macpherson, Graeme Nairn 2006

ISBN 0-9552201-0-6

Printed by MMS Almac Limited,
6 Tyock Industrial Estate, Elgin, Moray.

To all Scots fiddlers
who keep the heritage alive.
May this book inspire in
young musicians loyalty to
the traditional style.

Preface
by Fraser Macpherson

The process that led to the production of this book started in December 2003 when I visited the Royal Scottish Academy of Music and Drama with a view to archiving material I had relating to my father and his musical life. I had a moderate amount of photographs and newspaper clippings, programmes, a few musical scores, some old tapes and the most recent information about the "Macpherson fiddle", which had already been donated to the Academy.

It was Karen McAulay and Celia Duffy who examined what I had and who suggested, because of the intriguing historical elements of the material, that there was a story to be told.

My first thoughts were of a pamphlet or booklet, but it was not until I established contact with Bill Brian, an old friend of my father in the Scots fiddle scene in Elgin, that I became aware that we really had something to write about. Bill had preserved nearly all of my father's music, and, therefore, we had a record of some twenty tunes and much of the information about their titles and origins that our family had lost track of. Bill became a valuable contributor to the project, and we could never have achieved what we have without his involvement.

From this point the whole project grew, and I realised that I needed some professional help to do justice to the book. On the suggestion of Jackie Dewar, I found Richard Bennett and he led me to Graeme Nairn. Both had known Willie, through education and music, respectively, and both became very committed to what was beginning to evolve.

Once we got going, the project took on a life of its own, and it soon became clear to me that we were putting together a book of rare quality about Willie Macpherson, his music, his family life and the wonderful musical heritage he benefited from and contributed to.

Throughout the process I have been supported wholeheartedly by my wife Catriona, who has had to cope with me, by my sister Elizabeth, and by my brother Ian and his partner Donald McDowall-Wilson. Special thanks must also go to my cousin Evelyn Wiseman, her husband Allan and their son Allan and his partner Fiona. The enthusiasm and support of my family helped me enormously.

In addition to those mentioned above I must express my thanks to the following, all of whom contributed to the success of the project: James Alexander, Sylvia and Donald Alexander, Donald Barr, Katherine Campbell, Drummond and Carol Cook, Betty Cromarty, Stuart Eydmann, Inga and Sandy Gibb, Pamela Gillan, George Glasgow, Andrew Gracie, Margaret Heron, Erik Knussen, Bill Lees, Peter Lissauer, George MacDonald, Neil Macgregor, Mrs Muriel Macintyre, Seonaid Mackay, Charles Mackerron, Hilda Mackessack-Leitch, Ewen S L Macpherson, Jackie Macpherson, Mora Macpherson, Sandy Macpherson, Mr Sandy and Mrs Catherine Macpherson, Marion Marsh, Kirsteen Mitcalfe, J Murray Neil, Anne Oliver, Olive Ormiston, Bunty Patterson, Shirley Potts, Kim Planet, Mrs Helen Scott Robertson, Giulio Romano, Robbie Shepherd, Ronnie Steven, John Wallace, Graham Wilson, Jennifer Wilson, Graham Wiseman.

Special thanks must go to Johnstons of Elgin, in particular to James Dracup and Jenny Houldsworth.

Foreword
by Bill Brian

I first met Willie Macpherson at a Fiddle Festival in Kirriemuir in 1969. Willie was the adjudicator and I was one of the competitors. When the competitions had ceased for the day, Willie had been told that I was about to return to live in Elgin in my capacity as a draughtsman, working for the local Power Company, after having, like Willie, been away from my hometown for some years. He then introduced himself to me. In the course of our conversation that day, he indicated that he had in mind to revive the Elgin Strathspey and Reel Society, which had been in abeyance for some time. I told him I thought it was an excellent idea. At that point he asked me to be the leader of the reconstituted Society.

There started a friendship that lasted until Willie's untimely death in 1974. It was a wonderful five years friendship for me. What I learned from Willie in those years helped me greatly in my career as a musician. It was largely because of him and a mutual friend of us both, Peter Stewart from Lossiemouth, that I won the Golden Fiddle Award, the premier fiddling competition of the time.

What struck one when meeting Willie was his enthusiasm for life in general and for his music in particular, his fine wit and restlessness that was combined with a fierce determination. He was a person who was not happy unless he was challenging himself. Not content with that, he always felt it necessary to challenge his pupils and his musical friends - those of us who were willing to listen and learn.

This quality or trait is, I think, admirably demonstrated in the tunes that Willie composed. There is not a tune that one could say is "easy". I am reminded of a remark that William Marshall made regarding the degree of difficulty of the tunes he composed. He said that he did not write for bunglers, but in order to extend the capabilities of the fiddlers of his day. Although Willie never said so, I am sure he composed his tunes thinking very much along the same lines. All twenty are excellent tunes and there is something in all of them to challenge the keen amateur fiddle player.

The book describes Willie's personal life and musical life in some detail. It is an excellent story, well put together, and will, perhaps, go a long way to helping us understand what made Willie the man he was and the brilliant musician he proved to be. It is a story that needed to be told, and I commend the excellent work of Richard Bennett and Graeme Nairn for their research and gathering of details, bringing it all together and producing such a fine end result.

Willie's son, Fraser, who, it seems, has inherited the high level of enthusiasm, energy and that familiar restlessness of his father, should be commended for thinking up the idea of the book in the first place, kick-starting the whole thing off and managing to keep everything so well organised and controlled throughout.

It is a book long overdue but well worth waiting for.

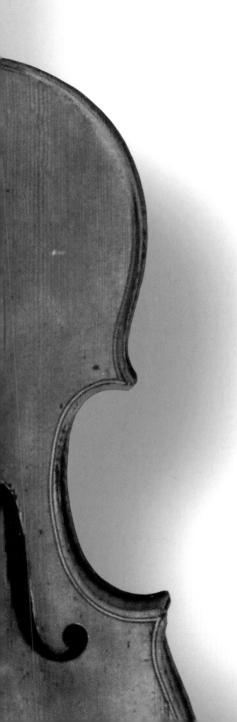

Contents

Chapter 1

The North East Tradition

The main weekly newspaper of this corner of the North East of Scotland, *The Northern Scot,* of 4 November 1972, carried, under the headline **TOWN HALL PACKED**, a review of the Elgin Strathspey and Reel Society's third annual Scots Concert. After a glowing account of various contributions, including the Senior Orchestra's "first rate fiddle playing of a very high standard", we find the following: "and now we come to Willie Macpherson's solos. Here was a classical player with quite lovely tone playing folk music in the traditional style. His fine technique showed to advantage in a splendid set of variations on the theme of *The Bluebells of Scotland* and, accompanied by Inga Gibb's most sensitive piano playing, this performance will long be remembered ... Willie Macpherson's name as a composer will undoubtedly join the ranks of Niel and Nathaniel Gow, Robert Mackintosh, William Marshall, Donald Grant, Charles Grant and Scott Skinner ... No country in the world has a wealth of folk music comparable to that of Scotland, and Elgin is indeed fortunate in having a young man so interested in fostering the traditional fiddling in our homeland".

The reviewer was Kim Murray, Willie Macpherson's music teacher since she was twentytwo and he was four years old. Kim's tribute is warm and her forecast of greatness for Willie as a composer is genuinely felt. But within a year and a half, Willie was dead. Kim Murray survived her pupil by nearly twelve years.

Kim Murray's list of noted fiddle composers is significant. All of these men made major contributions to the fiddle tradition of Scotland, and four of them came from or resided in Moray. William Marshall was born in Fochabers, Donald Grant lived in Elgin, Charles Grant came from Knockando, and James Scott Skinner married an Aberlour girl, lived in Elgin for twelve years and operated for much of his career in the area.

Of these, Marshall and Skinner are the best-known. Born in Fochabers in 1748 in poor circumstances, Marshall was a kind of universal genius of his time. Entering the service of the Duke of Gordon, he rapidly attained responsibility for administering the extensive household of Gordon Castle. After

some years he took on the farm of Keithmore, near Auchindoun Castle on the road to the Cabrach, and managed the Duke's extensive estates in that area. Later he and his wife retired to Newfield Cottage (now no longer in existence), near Dandaleith, on the west bank of the Spey at Craigellachie. Marshall was a professional man of wide interests - including, astronomy, architecture, clock-making and country sports - and, at the same time, the most accomplished musician of his day in Scotland. He was prosperous and comfortable and loved and admired, locally and nationally. Robert Burns described him as "the finest composer of strathspeys of his age". He published more than 250 tunes in his lifetime, his most important collection being the *Scottish Airs, Melodies, Strathspeys, Reels, &c* of 1822 which included such titles as *Archiestown*, *Balvenie Castle*, *Chapel Keithack*, *Craigellachie Bridge*, *Grant Lodge* and *Knockando House*. Marshall's fiddle technique was very distinctive, and his compositions make considerable demands on amateur fiddlers. He declared that he "did not write for bunglers" but in order to extend the capabilities of the fiddlers of his day. He died in 1833 and is buried in Bellie Cemetery.

Scott Skinner, on the other hand, born near Banchory in 1843, was a professional musician from the age of twelve, when he joined a touring band of boy players, "Dr Mark's Little Men", based in Manchester. He was soon winning major prizes for playing and for dancing and quickly became well-known as a dancing master and solo violinist in the North East. He married Jean Stewart, moved to Elgin and set up business at 2 South College Street in 1882, holding classes in the Assembly Rooms where "large numbers of young ladies and gentlemen gathered to learn the art of dancing". In November 1882, *The Moray and Nairn Express* reported: "Mr Scott Skinner is not nearly exhausted yet. His musical compilations are now nearly of weekly publication, and all present the same sprightliness of tune. The latest is *The Warbler's Polka*, dedicated to Mrs Johnston of Lesmurdie ..." Johnston's Mills, in Elgin, founded in 1800, was by this time a thriving concern. Skinner knew on which side his bread was buttered and freely named or dedicated tunes in order to gain sponsorship. Skinner was a businessman of prodigious energy, but, as it turned out, of little acumen - he opened dancing schools throughout the North, including in Forres, Nairn, Inverness, Dingwall, Invergordon, Tain and Wick, all towns accessible by rail. He was also a vastly prolific composer, and his second major collection of 59 tunes, *The Elgin Collection of Schottisches, Strathspeys, Reels, Hornpipes &c,* was published in 1884. The publication includes such titles as *Marshall's Style*, *Glenlivet*, *Miss Mary Jamieson of Elgin*, *Ladyhill*, *The Loch o' Drummuir*, *Miltonduff*, *The Banks o' Lossie* and *The Haughs o' Spey*, which bears the superscription:

"Dipple, Dundurcas, Dandaleith and Dalvey,
Are the bonniest haughs on the banks o' the Spey".

In his introduction to *The Elgin Collection,* Skinner writes: "the more I see and the more I become intimately acquainted with the picturesque, poetic and enchanting scenery of the Dee, Don, Deveron, Ythan, Ness and Spey, the greater I feel I am imbued with that class of music (ie. the Strathspey and Reel), for verily it is truly characteristic of the people and their manners in these quarters ..." That Skinner was well-acquainted in this area before establishing his base in Elgin is clear from some of the titles in his 1881 collection, *The Miller o' Hirn.* Such titles as *Castle Spynie*, *The Black Cat o' Ben Rinnes*, *Duncan on the Plainstanes*, *Lochnabo*, *Miss Johnston (Newmill)*, *Dr Whyte (Northview)*, *Bonnie Lossie* and *Glengrant* tell of close knowledge of the area as well as of his constant need to trawl for sponsorship. Skinner was hopeless with money and was declared bankrupt in 1885. In the same year he had his wife, Jean, committed to the Elgin Asylum at Bilbohall, and she remained there until her death in 1899, long after Skinner had left Elgin.

Rumour has it that he never visited his wife in Bilbohall and that he was pursued for many years by the authorities to provide financial support for her upkeep. A highly paid performer in the middle part of his career, Skinner was never able to save and he died in relative poverty in Aberdeen in 1927. He composed over 700 tunes, many of which became standards, he recorded prolifically and was known as The Strathspey King. His reputation is enormous today, although some purists argue that the continental flourishes he imported into his playing contributed to the corruption of authentic Scots fiddle playing.

Donald Grant (1760 - 1839) and Charles Grant (1806 - 1892) are lesser figures than these giants but still made important contributions to the continuity of the tradition of which Willie Macpherson was a part.

Little is known of the life of Donald Grant. He was born in Elgin and operated as a dancing master in the town. He was well-known in the area as a fiddler and composer and, in 1790, he published *A Collection of Airs, Strathspeys &c* which included such tunes as *The Earl of Moray's Reel* and *Darnaway Castle*.

Charles Grant, whose life straddled the Marshall-Skinner years, was born in Strondhu in Knockando of farming stock. He graduated from Aberdeen University and became a schoolteacher, first at Elchies and later at Aberlour School, where he remained for thirty years. He was an important figure in the Speyside community and was very highly regarded as an accomplished fiddler, composer and teacher of the fiddle. He was taught by William Marshall and received, as a gift from the family, following Marshall's death, one of the great man's fiddles. Later, he played with Scott Skinner. His compositions, published posthumously under the title *Strathspeys, Reels, Pibrochs and Marches*, include such well-known melodies as *Ben Rinnes*, *Mrs Jamieson's Favourite*, *Railway Hornpipe*, *Swiss Cottage (Ballindalloch)*, *Dellagyle* and *Poolachrie*. The last two titles, being the names of salmon pools on the Spey, reveal Grant's passion for fishing.

The Moray contribution to the North East fiddle tradition has been significant. The continuity of that contribution can be traced from the early days of Marshall and Grant to Scott Skinner in the first quarter of last century. When Skinner died in 1927, Willie Macpherson was seven years old and already performing to a high level.

Chapter 2

The Family

Willie Macpherson was born into an Elgin family of prodigious musical ability. Of the seven surviving children of James and Sophia Macpherson, five became professional musicians. The three boys, Ernest, Willie and Richard (Dickie), earned their livings almost exclusively in the musical world, and two of the girls, Margaret (Meggie) and Ethel, supplemented their wages by playing in bands, by teaching and by accompanying dancers. The musical environment in which the children grew up was intense. Their father was a musician, a member of the Elgin City Band (and later Bandmaster). He was a hard taskmaster, expectations were high, and, although money was short, music lessons were paid for for all the children from an early age.

Where did this remarkable flowering of musical talent come from? Who knows? The children's mother Sophia had no music in her family. James "Neefie" Macpherson was the son of an Elgin girl who had, in the 1880s, left Elgin to work as a chambermaid in the Caledonian Hotel in Edinburgh and returned in 1885 to have her child. After leaving the East End School, James found work at Johnston's Mill, where he remained as weaver and pattern maker for the rest of his life. That he was imbued with a love of music is certain. A persistent family legend links his conception with a visit to Edinburgh of the great Italian conductor, Arturo Toscanini, but the legend is based on a perceived facial resemblance rather than on hard facts. However, Toscanini was a

notorious ladies' man: "I smoked my first cigarette and kissed my first girl on the same day," he said, "and I've never smoked since" ...

At any rate the young Jimmy Macpherson was an entirely self-taught musician. He taught himself to play the cornet and the violin, fingering the violin in a very peculiar way with his fingers above the strings as if he were playing the cornet. He played in the Elgin City Silver Band for many years and was Bandmaster from 1935 to 1947 when he retired on health grounds. He also played in dance bands. Often he would complete a ten-hour day at his skilled and demanding job at the mill, change into evening dress and head out to play

until he returned home at two am only to get up at six to start work again. He was a perfectionist in everything he tried to achieve and demanded a lot of his children - especially with regard to their music. He was devoted to his children and grandchildren, and they to him. He died in 1954.

The family lived around the east end of Elgin, moving accommodation as the family grew and diminished. The eldest surviving son, Ernest, (b.1906) - they lost a son, James, in infancy - and daughter, Effie, (b.1908), were born at 23 Collie Street. The Macphersons then moved to 31B High Street, Forteath's Close, where the next four children, Meggie (b.1913), Ethel (b.1916), Willie (b.1920) and Dickie (b.1923), were born. The last child, Adela, was born in one of the new Turriff Bungalows at 12 East Road in 1929. There were further moves - to 10 Pansport Place and later to 90 South College Street, where Jimmy died. Sophia then moved to 16 East Road where she died in 1957.

All the children attended the East End School. Only Willie, and Adela went on to Elgin Academy, the others completing their secondary education at the East End.

The first to show outstanding musical ability was Ernest. Under the sobriquet "Wee Mac", Ernest, we are told, was charming concert audiences with his violin playing at the age of five. *The Northern Scot Christmas Number* of 1921 shows a photograph with the caption, "Master Ernest Macpherson, a 15 year old Elgin violinist who gives promise of a distinguished career." There were no grants or bursaries to support promising young talent in those days, but the musical world of Elgin - and Ernest Macpherson in particular - was extremely fortunate in having two remarkably generous patrons: Mrs Rose Mackessack of Ardgye and Colonel W. J. Johnston of Lesmurdie. Clearly, Elgin could not provide the musical education that exceptional talent demanded in order to progress, and these two benefactors were principally responsible for paying for Ernest to go to study, first, at the Royal College of Music in London and then to Berlin, to train under the world-famous virtuoso and teacher, Carl Flesch. We can hardly guess what it was like for a young Elgin loon to find himself living in Germany in the 1920s but we can imagine the extraordinary pride that his parents must have felt at the privilege. In Berlin, Ernest met Gretchen, the girl he was to marry and was soon embarked on a fulltime musical career. In the early 1930s, he joined the violins of the embryonic BBC Theatre Orchestra, under Stanford Robinson. This orchestra was essentially a radio orchestra, providing incidental music for dramatic productions, appearing on variety programmes and performing its own light music concerts. Gradually, the role of the orchestra changed under Robinson, the amount of light music was limited and it became, in effect, a second BBC symphony orchestra. The name was changed to the BBC Concert Orchestra in 1952. After a full and rich career of thirty years at the BBC, Ernest left the Orchestra in 1962 to take up the post of Head of the Music Department at Beath High School in Fife where he remained until his retirement. He also taught part-time at the Carnegie Music Institute in Dunfermline. Ernest died in 1972.

The girls, Meggie (1913 - 1988) and Ethel (1916 - 1978), were both accomplished musicians who were well known in the area. They played in bands and performed accompaniments. In the early part of her career, Meggie played for "Tihi" Dunbar's Dancing School and, on leaving Elgin to live in Aberdeen, performed a similar function there for Miss Birse's Dancing School. Also in Aberdeen, in the early 1950s, she accompanied Willie, played with him in the band at the Caledonian Hotel and did some work for the BBC.

The musical career of Dickie was remarkable. A trumpet player, his talent was for the swing music and big band jazz of the 1930s, '40s, '50s. Following the War, during which he was a tail-gunner in Lancasters, playing his trumpet on the way home from bombing raids, he was "discovered" by the well-known jazz journalist, Steve Race, and joined the Carl Barriteau Band at the Eldorado Ballroom in Leith. Later he played with the Vic Lewis and Ken Macintosh Bands and toured the world several times, accompanying such greats as Johnny Ray, Ella Fitzgerald and Louis Armstrong. In the late 1950s, he moved to the world of pop music, joining Don Lang's Frantic Five and figuring regularly on the first of the pop music programmes on television, *Six Five Special.* He then entered management, acting as Musical Director for such as Shirley Bassey and P. J. Proby. He also guested at the *Two Red Shoes* in Elgin on visits to the North. Dickie died in 2001.

Chapter 3

The Early Years

The early career of Willie Macpherson is well recorded in family photographs and in the local press. Taught initially by his father, he became a pupil of the well-known Elgin music teacher, Miss Kim Murray, at the age of four. By the time he was eight he was playing solos in Kim Murray's concerts and was established in her Junior String Ensemble. In the Town Hall Concert of 7 March 1928 in aid of funds for Dr Gray's Hospital, he played Beethoven's *Minuet* and Jessop's *Gavotte*. In 1930, the *Press and Journal* reported of his playing at the Banffshire Music Festival: "here was a violinist of a very high standard, and still greater promise. It was a very remarkable achievement for a lad who has just passed his tenth birthday". The *Elgin Courant* of 26th January 1934 previews Kim Murray's Annual Concert as follows: "the 'Piece de Resistance' is undoubtedly the Mendelssohn Violin Concerto in which Willie Macpherson, so well-known to Elgin audiences, will play the solo part. This is an ambitious undertaking for anyone, but for a boy of 14 it is doubly so, and it rebounds to his pluck and to the confidence of his teacher that he is able to attempt this difficult Concerto". And, indeed, an extraordinarily ambitious undertaking for an exclusively amateur orchestra in a small country

town. In May 1934, Willie won classes in both classical and traditional playing at the prestigious Northern Counties Musical Festival in Inverness.

That the musical scene in Elgin was flourishing is evident from the details of the concert of November 1935. Kim Murray's Junior Orchestra comprising eighty "very keen youngsters" accompanied a choir of ninety vocalists. The Senior Orchestra played Mozart's Violin Concerto with Willie Macpherson playing the solo part. In addition, the Senior Orchestra, led by Willie, played a Scots Suite, written for strings by Colonel Johnston of Lesmurdie. The *Courant* comments: "[Colonel Johnston's] interest and work for music locally is so well known and appreciated by all. The Suite has received high praise and is shortly going to be played by a London orchestra. Here we are to have it in his own home town with the composer himself playing the viola in the orchestra".

A word about Kim Murray. Born in Elgin in 1902, Kathleen Ida Murray (hence "Kim") taught music, specialising in violin and piano, in her home town almost all her life. She studied first under her mother and, after completing her normal schooling at Elgin Academy, she attended the Royal Academy of Music in London, graduating with distinction as an Associate of the Academy (ARAM). She threw herself into her teaching work in Elgin and took a prominent part, along with her pupils, in establishing the Moray Music Festival

as a major event in the North. She was fiercely demanding but was much loved and enjoyed enormous success as a teacher. The works she selected for public performance were evidence of her extraordinary confidence and ambition. She organised and played in orchestras and string quartets and - Burghead was an active BBC station at the time - made many radio broadcasts with her pupils, often live from the Assembly Rooms on the corner of High Street and North Street or from the BBC studio in Lossie Wynd. During the Second World War, she did sterling work in entertaining members of the Forces stationed in the area. She taught Prince Charles the 'cello while he was a pupil at Gordonston. She was awarded the MBE in 1971. She died in 1986.

Over a period of more than sixty years, thousands of young people in Elgin and the surrounding area owed a great deal to Kim Murray. She had many outstanding pupils, but, at the same time in the mid-1930s, she had under her tutelage three who were very special to her. Willie Macpherson may have been top of the list but, just a little younger than Willie, and very close to him in terms of musical talent, were Jimmy and Ella Taylor from Barmuckity. Kim Murray moved mountains to provide these three with the financial support necessary to further their musical education.

London was the Mecca for musicians. Kim organised concerts in order to raise funds to finance her young proteges. In the *Courant* of 28

January 1935, she wrote: "my object for these young players giving recitals is to add to the fund already begun for their musical education when they will require to go further afield". In the *Courant* of 19 September 1936, she wrote: "the time has now come for these very talented young Elgin musicians to go to London to further their musical education. All three have been successful in gaining grants of a small sum of money annually, and I hope this may be augmented as time goes on". Colonel Johnston of Lesmurdie supported her appeal: "I would like to add my hope that the Morayshire public will do what they can to help these very gifted children ... It is no exaggeration to say that their talent and executive powers are quite out of the ordinary ... It is up to the people of Moray to see that these children get a full opportunity of bringing their undoubted talent to fruition". The report of the recital, which was a great success, states: "Elgin has followed with interest the musical career of the young people, following them through their initial stages, watching the maturing of their playing, the added depth of tone, the more finished technique, that crispness and neatness of playing that comes from experience ..." Items played included Beethoven's String Quartet Op 29 and Mozart's String Quartet in D Major. The children were accompanied in these pieces by Miss Murray, Colonel Johnston and Mr John Geddes. The review, which incidentally criticises Willie's solo playing for lack of "the care and precision that it had when he was younger", heaps praise on the efforts of the "two great benefactors" and expresses the hope that "in the wider sphere of their new life in London these young people will not forget them". The fact that, within a few years, following success in London, all three returned to Elgin to help Kim with her teaching is testimony to the fact that they did not forget.

A very important gift that was to have an enormous influence on the ultimate career of Willie Macpherson received no public mention anywhere - probably at the request of the benefactor. She was Mrs Rose Mackessack of Ardgye, who had earlier contributed to Ernest's musical education, and the gift, made to Willie when he was fifteen, was a violin of exceptional quality. It is unlikely that the Mackessacks knew just how special it was, but that instrument was to be Willie's livelihood for the next forty years. The story of the violin is told later.

The *Courant* of 8 January 1937 tells us that "Willie Macpherson, for the last time before leaving to further his musical education in London, led the Elgin Senior orchestra at last night's concert". How long Willie stayed in London, how he found the teaching, who his teachers were, how he enjoyed London is not known. At any rate he was back in Elgin leading Kim Murray's Orchestra in the January Concert of 1938. The *Courant* of 6 January 1939 carries, under the headline **HONOURS DEGREE FOR TALENTED YOUNG ELGIN VIOLINIST,** the following report: "we have to congratulate Mr Willie Macpherson ... on the degree of Licentiate of the College of Violinists which has just been conferred on him with Honours... During the last year, Mr Macpherson has been trained in teaching methods and has been a pupil of Mr Alwyne A. Laxton for Harmony, in which subject he gained very high marks in the degree examination". Alwyne Laxton (or Joe, as he was known by generations of schoolchildren) spent his whole career teaching in the area and was for many years Head of the Music Department at Elgin Academy. And so it is clear that some of the teaching towards Willie's degree took place in Elgin. In fact he was back at home helping Kim Murray with her teaching load while working towards the completion of his degree.

In the annual Concert of March 1939, Willie is recorded as being leader of the first violins and as conductor of the "Reel and Strathspey Band of Boys".

Although she loved Scots music and prepared pupils for traditional music classes in festivals, Kim never specialised in teaching it; for her orchestras, traditional music tended to be a late "add on" to the Classical repertoire and she may well have been very glad to make use of Willie's enthusiasm to cater for the wide interest in the area for the style.

At the age of nineteen Willie may have had some idea of a future career: he had a much admired talent, he had a superb instrument, he had undergone a very high level of musical education, he was qualified to teach. The musical world was open to him.

And then the War came, and for Willie, as for many millions of others, everything changed for ever.

Chapter 4

The War Years and After

By many people's standards Willie Macpherson had an easy War. He joined the RAF ground staff in 1940, was trained as an Airframe Fitter, and, in early 1941, was posted to Mt Hampton RAF base in Southern Rhodesia (now Zimbabwe). There his musical talents came to the fore and were nurtured. He played for the forces and for the

extremely hospitable locals. He made many friends, including "Professor" Jimmy Edwards, the comedian and trombonist, who later won the DFC at Arnhem. He played and broadcast solos, in string trios and quartets and in orchestras. He and a Viennese musician broadcast a Bach Double Violin Concerto. For the benefit of the many Scots in Southern Rhodesia, the Burns Night Celebrations in the capital, Salisbury, were broadcast. Special mention was made of Willie's contributions in the press. An article in the Elgin *Courant* of 7 July 1942 - the local press was always keen to print news of Moray loons abroad - states: "always a keen footballer, Willie Macpherson is a prominent forward line player in the RAF team. While in the Dominion, he has made the acquaintance of another native of Moray - Mr A. R. Taylor, formerly Maths master at Elgin Academy, who belongs to Lhanbryde. In a letter to his parents, Willie tells of the kindness bestowed upon him by Mr and Mrs Taylor, who have put a room at his disposal to practise in and, in Willie's own words, 'treat him like a son'".The piece ends: "the community will join us in sending best wishes to Mr Macpherson for a speedy return to his homeland and to the furtherment of his career".

Events that followed the end of the War lend an ironic twist to the last remark. For Willie, as did many members of His Majesty's Forces returning to civvy street in 1946, found life very hard.

In 1939, at the age of 19,Willie had married Betty Fraser, a hairdresser, who lived at 50 East High Street, Bishopmill. They moved in with Betty's parents.The family came. Fraser was born in 1940,

Ian in 1945 and Elizabeth in 1948.After the War, the growing family moved into their own accommodation, first at 45 East High Street then in Burghead where Betty opened a small hairdressing business. For Willie, finding employment was difficult. His former colleague, Ella Taylor, filled the post of assistant to Kim Murray. And Willie was a musician; that was his training, and, in the post-war years in Elgin, opportunities were very few. Except, that is, in the field of dance music. In those years of austerity, dancing was enormously popular. On any Friday or Saturday night there could be as many as a dozen dances within a few miles' radius of Elgin. On a typical weekend in November 1946, the local press advertised dances, in Elgin, at the Lido Ballroom (with "Johnnie Thompson and his Professional Orchestra, Playing Pleasing Music and Perfect Tempo at all Sessions - up to date buffet serving hot and cold snacks"), at the Assembly

Rooms, the Drill Hall, East End School, Bishopmill Hall, in Lossiemouth at the Stotfield Hotel, The British Legion Hall, and at halls at Fogwatt, Hopeman, Spynie, Lhanbryde, Miltonduff, Archiestown, Garmouth, Spey Bay, Urquhart, Inchberry and Pluscarden. Never, before or since, have these country halls seen such action. There were three Schools of Dancing in Elgin, including Cliff Scott's at the "Super New Lido", teaching principally Ballroom. There were even *Dancing Notes,* written by Jack Cruickshank, in the weekly press. There we find such gems as: "overheard in an Elgin Dance Hall, 'I would rather dance all evening with a girl standing on my toes than have a few minutes on the floor with one persistently chewing gum!' How true that is!". We also find, in December 1946, the following report, so evocative of the times and with a connection to the Macpherson story: "latest singing star to face the bright lights and the microphone in the Bishopmill Hall was 15 year old Jackie Macpherson, whose rendering of popular songs of today,

alternately in typical 'Frankie' and 'Bing' style, had the bobbysoxers standing with mouths open. Jackie, the Singing Message Boy, is well-known in Elgin, and his style of putting over songs has got a real touch of class about it". Jackie was Willie's nephew and lived with his grandparents, Jimmy and Sophia at 90 South College Street.

It is also in this column that we find, on 1 November, 1946, the following: "a new dance band formed in Elgin is that of Willie Macpherson (of Bishopmill) and his Music". "Willie Macpherson and his Music" became the resident band at the Marine and Stotfield Hotels in Lossiemouth, playing at the bi-weekly Dinner Dances, while a trio regularly accompanied diners at lunch, dinner and afternoon tea. There were also engagements for the band at dances and balls in the Assembly Rooms: for the Freemasons, The Unionist Party, St Sylvester's Fabric Fund, The Young People from the Occupied Countries Reception Committee. But the income was not enough to support a growing family, even with the contribution from Betty's hairdressing salon. There were not the openings in the Elgin area for Willie's career as a musician to develop. His talent was wasted playing dance music. A decision had to be taken and, in 1948, the family moved to Aberdeen. Opportunities for playing were greater: Willie played in the theatre orchestra, in bands and orchestras put together for particular events and in the resident band at the Caledonian Hotel, where his sister, Meggie, joined him for a period when she moved with her family to Aberdeen. He played across the North with the Scottish Country Dance Band led by Annie Shand Scott and was often called upon to play, both as a soloist and in groups, at the BBC Scotland studios in the city. He also had a fulltime job as an assistant Sacrist (a kind of janitor) at Marischal College in the University of Aberdeen and was pleased to meet his old wartime mate, Jimmy Edwards, when Jimmy was elected Lord Rector of the University in the early 1950s.

The stresses of such a lifestyle told on Willie. He was playing music night after night in a wide variety of modes but at a cost. In 1954 he left his job and the family in Aberdeen and went to look for work in Edinburgh. There he led orchestras in the George Hotel and in Peebles Hydro for a season.

These had been a difficult fifteen years during which Willie's career had not progressed, but, despite the day-to-day shifting of styles - from Scottish to Classical to Quickstep and Rhumba - neither his talent nor his appetite for playing had diminished, and soon everything was to change again.

In 1955 Willie auditioned for the Scottish National Orchestra and was accepted straight into the First Violins.

Chapter 5

The SNO Years

The move, for Willie, in 1955 from being essentially a jobbing musician, playing anything in any style, anywhere, to being a fulltime member of the First Violins in a major, national symphony orchestra was dramatic. The commitment demanded was total, and the money was good. After a hiatus of fifteen years, at the age of thirtyfive, Willie's career as a professional musician was on track. There was a change of life for the family. They moved to Glasgow, the home of the SNO, to 231 Danes Drive, Scotstoun, where they remained for the next eleven years. Fraser had left school by this time and was working as an apprentice electrician. Ian and Elizabeth settled into secondary school at Victoria Drive School, Scotstoun, and Betty went back to hairdressing.

The Scottish National Orchestra had been established on a permanent basis in 1950 with a mission to provide orchestral music throughout Scotland all the year round. The SNO was, in fact, the first orchestra in the whole country to pay its musicians on a fixed annual salary rather than on short term, sometimes seasonal, contracts. The Orchestra was required by the terms of its foundation to take its national responsibility seriously and it regularly travelled to those towns - only four outside the major cities in the mid-fifties - that had halls suitable to accommodate it. It did not come to Elgin until the new Sir Basil Spence-designed Town Hall was opened in 1961. (The Victorian Town Hall in which Willie had performed with Kim Murray's Orchestra as a boy

had been burned down in 1939.) The requirement to travel and the heavy concert programme made demands on the musicians. In the 1962-63 season, for example, the Orchestra played 179 concerts - more than three a week - and, outside Glasgow, Edinburgh, Aberdeen and Dundee, played in fourteen towns across the country. The Orchestra's Prospectus for the 1958-59 season shows a repertoire of ninetyfour major works that comprised the programmes for the weekly Saturday evening concerts in the St Andrews Hall. The midweek concerts had a different repertoire. The Orchestra moved to the Glasgow Concert Hall - to considerable loss of revenue because of a much smaller seating capacity - when the St Andrews Hall burned down in 1962.

First Violins
Sam Bor, *Leader*
Herbert Whone, *Deputy Leader*
Douglas Reid
∗ Jean Rennie
∗ Leonard Davis
Dorothie Sawtell
∗ Leonard Fish
William Macpherson
Margaret Ackroyd
William Brown
Maureen Dickinson
∗ Carlos Bertelli

It is a measure of Willie's remarkable talent that he was able to move comfortably from the hand-to-mouth, Jack-of-all-trades musical life that had been his lot for the last fifteen years to the rarified and intense musical life of a major national symphony orchestra involving two or three concerts a week and many hours of rehearsal
.

The three Principal Conductors who spanned Willie's career at the SNO were Karl Rankl, who was followed by another famous Austrian, Hans Swarowsky, until the appointment, in 1959, of Alexander Gibson, the first Scot to hold the post. Always affable and convivial, Willie contributed significantly to the life of the Orchestra; he helped to lighten the tension and the tedium of lengthy

rehearsal sessions and he made many friends, among them Giulio Romano, of the 'cellos and the tuba player and Orchestra Manager, Erik Knussen, both of whom remember Willie with great affection.

During these years, Willie played with all the world's greatest musicians who were guest soloists with the Orchestra. Among these was one with whom Willie established a particular rapport and a friendship that lasted well after Willie had left the SNO. Yehudi Menuhin (later, Lord Menuhin) was an iconic figure to all violinists. From a very early age his performances had been rapturously received but he was never just a musician; he wanted, as he said, "to make his music work for humanity". He was also keen to experiment and played duets with Stephane Grappelli, the jazz violinist, and with Ravi Shankar, the renowned sitar player, who brought his instrument to the attention of the West. When playing with the SNO in January 1962, Menuhin expressed an interest in the Scots fiddle tradition and there followed a series of masterclasses, with Willie as master and Menuhin as pupil, playing and listening to tunes and observing and analysing closely the distinctive fingering and bowing techniques of the style. Menuhin's interest was not transitory. The two corresponded and Willie sent him books of fiddle music and copies of tunes. Menuhin became sufficiently expert in the traditional music of Scotland to be invited to act as a judge in the BBC Scotland Scots Fiddle-playing Competition in 1969, in which Willie took part. Curiously, Menuhin played in a concert in the Fochabers Institute as part of the village's Bicentenary celebrations in 1976.

Willie had, throughout the SNO years, maintained contact with the world of traditional music. As well as doing work for BBC Scotland, taking part in traditional music programmes, providing background music for documentaries with a Scottish theme and so on, he was often called on to do solo work on special occasions. *The Scotsman* reports a programme of Scottish verse and music at the Edinburgh International Festival in 1961 as follows (the reviewer takes the opportunity to have a swipe at Schoenberg, whose work dominated the Festival that year): "the fiddle music played by William Macpherson, with no sort of apology to the atonal Mr Sch... haunting the place these days, was very warmly received. This is the kind of stuff which, if its indigenous like were discovered in some far-off corner of Europe, would send foreign critics away home writing rave notices. It was 'halesome farin'' that could hold up its head honourably anywhere." Willie also made a number of recordings with the Park Film Studio Players in Glasgow. The sleeve notes on a series of EPs entitled *Dances of Scotland,* made with James Burnett on guitar and James Robertson on double bass, conclude with the following: "the greatest early exponents of the art were Niel and Nathaniel Gow. William Marshall and Scott Skinner were worthy successors and today the tradition is continued by a group of musicians, in which William Macpherson must be included".

Willie's years with the SNO came to an end in 1966, and he returned to Elgin to throw himself into teaching his instrument and to helping revive the Scots fiddle tradition in the area.

Chapter 6

The Fiddle

When, in 1784, Pate Baillie stole Niel Gow's fiddle in the streets of Edinburgh, and Gow pursued and caught the thief, the old fiddler admonished him: "whatever ye dae, dinna try to steal a man's fiddle; ye micht as weel steal his bairn".

A major part of Willie Macpherson's success as a musician was the instrument he received as a gift at the age of fifteen and which remained with him for the rest of his life.

The donor of the fiddle was Mrs Rose Mackessack of Ardgye and, later, of Hythehill, West High Street, Bishopmill. Mrs Mackessack was the wife of George Mackessack and the mother of Colonel Kenneth Mackessack of Ardgye and of Major Douglas Mackessack of Inverugie. She was the daughter of Major Grant of Glen Grant, Rothes. When she died in 1960 at the age of eighty two, she was described in the press as the "much-loved Elgin lady, well-known for her ardent work in connection with charitable and welfare organisations". She was founder of the Moray Nursing Association and the first County Commissioner of Guides; she was founder President of both Alves and Bishopmill WRIs. She was also extremely musical and had studied piano alongside Eileen Joyce in her youth and she was very committed to supporting the development of music in the Moray area. She had contributed significantly to the fund set up to enable Willie's brother, Ernest, to study, first in London and, later, in Berlin.

Members of Mrs Mackessack's family are unsure of the origins of the instrument but think it most likely that she had, recognising something of its quality, bought it in the South for the purpose of donating it to a worthy recipient in Moray - perhaps even to Willie himself.

This was an extraordinarily generous gift to a boy of fifteen, for this is a remarkable instrument of rare beauty and tone. Originally thought to be of Genoese origin, recent research suggests it to be an English instrument. David Rattray, Curator of the String Instrument Collection of the Royal Academy of Music in London, writes: "the instrument appears to be English, circa 1760, and is close in style to the work of Joseph Hill, although I am unable with certainty to give a maker's name to the instrument. English characteristics include the square single chamfered lining and also the shape of the blocks. In addition I did notice that the top block has a nail hole indicating the original method of neck attachment. I could see why the instrument may have been confused with Italian work. In fact it does have characteristics of the Florentine school, in particular, the full arching and gold coloured varnish. However, under black light the quality appears to be an English type".

The relationship between a professional musician and his or her instrument is complex - intense, emotional, perhaps unique in human experience, and impossible for a non-musician to understand. The instrument may be, as in this case, a thing of beauty, a work of art that is capable of creating art, of giving exquisite pleasure, and it is, at the same time, the means of paying the mortgage and of feeding and clothing the children. This violin was created when Mozart was a toddler and at least ten years before Beethoven was born. It would be interesting to know of the relationships which this instrument had been part of in the 170 or so years of its existence before

Amira Bedrush-McDonald is th

Macphers

JIM MCBETH

EVEN in a building where the sound of music is common-place, the violin   ne is in
class of it
from '

it was entrusted to Willie Macpherson's care and became, for the next forty years, his constant and cherished companion and the means of livelihood for him and his family.

Following his death in 1974, the instrument passed into the care of Willie's eldest child, Fraser. He knew that such an instrument should not remain idle. He arranged for it to be used by a family friend, the well-known tenor David Dyer, as a "second instrument" while studying at the Royal Scottish Academy of Music and Drama in the late 1970s. It was then on loan to the Scottish National Orchestra for four or five years from 1982. It was returned to the family when senior managers of the orchestra, who had known Willie and had known the violin, retired and felt that, in their absence, it might not receive the care and attention it merited. However, the family were always very conscious of the fact that the violin did not really belong to them: it had been a gift to their father, placed in his trust and, subsequently, in their trust. On their mother's death in 2002, they opened negotiations with the Royal Scottish Academy of Music and Drama to have the instrument restored and to find it a permanent home where it would be played by musicians who could respond to its quality. The terms of the final agreement reached with RSAMD state that: " the violin was donated ... so that future generations of students who are in need of a good instrument but have no resources to purchase one, may use the instrument while studying... Students will be

lent to play the Macpherson violin, which has been donated to the academy.　　Picture: Robert Per

iolin airs new life in its strings

strument.　hands of Ms Bedrush-
lin was as　McDonald, 21, who won a com-
　　petition to play it, it is beyond
value.
　　Macpherson was born i

violinist's son, said: "It's true
value, in the hands of a talented
musician, is beyond price. One
of my treasured possessions is a
of dad with Yehudi

who also plays in a ceilidh ba
in her spare time.
　　She said: "I'm delighted
panel of judges pick
have it

selected by the Head of Strings by competition... Though not a condition, it would be appreciated if, from time to time, the selected student was involved in the Scottish Music scene ..." The Macphersons also agreed to make an annual donation to help the Academy in future restoration of the violin and other stringed instruments. The first recipients of the instrument were Stephanie Brough and Amira Bedrush-Mcdonald and, most recently, for 2005-6, the talented young musician from the Isle of Man, Katie Stone.

When the instrument was handed over to the Academy in March 2004, the Head of Strings, Peter Lissauer, declared: "this violin is an invaluable resource to us ... This particular instrument has so much heritage that it inspires the students ... It is the Crown Jewel in the Academy's collection of strings".

The purpose of the Macpherson family in making this donation was twofold: as well as creating a memorial to their father, they wanted to pass on, in trust, to future generations of young musicians in Scotland the remarkable gift from the original benefactor - Mrs Rose Mackessack of Ardgye - that had so enhanced their father's life and career.

Chapter 7

Elgin Again

The return of Willie Macpherson to Elgin in 1966 caused a mild stir. It was reported in the press, and the word went round. Although he had been away from the place for sixteen years, the parts he had played in the local music scene were fresh in the memory, and his career and those of his brothers had been followed with interest. He and Betty settled at 36 Blantyre Place in Bishopmill and, by early 1967, Willie had become established as a music teacher with the local authority.

Around this time, the Joint County Council of Moray and Nairn had put in place a system whereby pupils with some musical ability could receive instrumental tuition through the schools. Graham Wiseman was appointed County Music Organiser and he soon recognised the contribution that a musician of Willie's quality and experience could bring to the scheme. Willie also brought his experience of orchestral playing to bear on local concert giving. He led orchestras for many ambitious concerts conducted by Graham Wiseman. Ella Taylor, Willie's playing companion of thirty years earlier, joined the staff to teach 'cello, and soon she and Willie joined up with their former teacher, Kim Murray, Inga Gibb and Ronnie Stevens to play string quartets and quintets every Sunday afternoon.

Willie's teaching for the local authority focused on Lossiemouth High School, Forres Academy and Milne's High School. He also contributed to the Saturday morning music school and to a series of intensive, week-long, residential orchestral courses held at Grantown Grammar School in July. (Grantown-on-Spey was, at that time, in the county of Moray.) He also drew a number of private pupils from a wide area who came to benefit from his gifts of musicianship and of teaching. He was a patient, gentle teacher who communicated to his pupils both his understanding of and his love for the instrument.

Willie was, at this time, also practising and composing traditional fiddle music and playing informally with the players who were to become the nucleus of the re-formed Elgin Strathspey and Reel Society.

In 1969, he entered the BBC Scotland Scots Fiddle-playing Competition. There were 116 entries from all over the British Isles. Preliminary rounds were held in four centres, including Aberdeen, and Willie was among the six selected to play in the Final, held in Perth City Halls on 28 November 1969. Competition was tough. The finalists included, apart from Willie, three very well-known and experienced musicians: Angus Cameron, from Kirriemuir, Charles Cowie, from Glasgow, and Arthur Scott Robertson, from Shetland. The other two competitors were the relatively inexperienced Florence Burns, from Aberdeen, and John Morrison, from Kintore. The adjudicators were Hector Macandrew, James Hunter, Watson Forbes and Yehudi Menuhin, who had been helped to extend his understanding of the Scots tradition by Willie back in 1962. The contestants had to play four widely varying groups of pieces, some of their own choice, some from a specially compiled booklet. Willie's selection was as follows: March, Strathspey and Reel - *Leaving Glenurquhart*, *Laird o' Drumblair*, *High Road to Linton*, the Slow Air - *The Valley of Silence*, the Slow Strathspey and Reel - *Mackworth* and *Mary*

Walker, the Slow Strathspey and Hornpipe, his own compositions, both entitled *Effie Glasgow of Longmorn*. Willie's friend, Mrs Glasgow was in the audience.

In the end Willie won the second prize of £50, behind the Shetland fiddler, Arthur Robertson. In conversation afterwards, Yehudi Menuhin told him that the judges had considered his playing to be "too fine" to merit first place. Whatever Menuhin meant by that, Willie was delighted to come second in such company.

Willie now threw his energies into reviving the Elgin Strathspey and Reel Society that had been in abeyance since the early 1950s. He was lucky to have, as his partner in this enterprise, Bill Brian, the highly talented musician - and former pupil of Kim Murray - who had returned to Elgin in 1969. An inaugural meeting was held in the Glasgows' house at Longmorn Distillery in January 1970, and Willie was elected President and Musical Director. Interest and membership grew rapidly, and the Society gave twenty concerts in the course of its first year.

BBC SCOTLAND

SCOTS FIDDLE - PLAYING COMPETITION FINAL

PERTH   NOVEMBER   1969

Willie was an inspiration as a conductor. His presence attracted the best players, including a number of young players of high ability - Charles McKerron, Douglas Lawrence, Kenneth Lindsay, Shirley Potts, Stuart Huyton - and he had the knack of eliciting the best from his players.

Willie was a traditionalist in terms of the sound he wanted to produce. He had no time for the accordians and guitars with which some Societies augmented the fiddles. It was the pure, sometimes ethereal, sound that his own instrument could

create that he strove for - and achieved. Soon, members of the Society were winning competitions and classes across the North East, and, in 1972, the Society won the orchestral competitions in the festivals at Banchory and Kirriemuir. The Society's first festival in Elgin in 1972 attracted a hundred individual competitors and seven orchestras from all over Scotland. The traditional music scene was once again established in Moray and was going from strength to strength. It was Willie Macpherson who was responsible for its revival.

In many ways these years were the happiest time of Willie's life. He was a natural teacher: he loved teaching, and his pupils loved him and were inspired by him. His playing had lost none of its verve or brilliance or beauty of tone. He was busy: one weekend he could be conducting in a Scots Concert and playing exquisite solos; the next, leading the orchestra in a full-length performance of Handel's *Messiah*. He was playing music of both kinds for pleasure with good and old friends. But the happiness of these years was to be short-lived.

The musical world that Willie had inhabited from an early age was intensely creative, draining of personal resources - and extremely sociable. In his early fifties, the strain began to tell. The congenital heart disease that had cut short the lives of a number of the Macpherson family struck. His youngest sister, Adela, had died a year or so earlier at the age of fortytwo, leaving five children. In the spring of 1974, Willie fell ill. He was in and out of hospital for some months.

His last public performance as musician and as teacher was an auspicious one. In 1974 the 750th anniversary of the foundation of Elgin Cathedral was marked in the town by a series of events. On 6 July, the Moray and Nairn Schools' Orchestra played a Concert in Elgin Town Hall. One hundred and ten instrumental pupils had been in residence in Grantown for an intensive week's rehearsals prior to the performance. The Concert programme was extremely demanding: Gordon Jacob's *A Noyse of Minstrells* was followed by Elgar's *Nimrod* from *Enigma Variations,* Albinoni's *Sonata in E Minor* and the fourth movement of *Symphonie Fantastique* by Berlioz. The Concert concluded with the specially commissioned piece by David Stone, the *Sinfonietta for Orchestra and Brass Band*, described by one of the participants as "fiendishly difficult".

Remarkably, given the state of his health, Willie played a full part in the rehearsals in Grantown and in the performance itself - along with the friends and colleagues he had known for so long: Ella and Jimmy Taylor, Drummond Cook, Keith Fisher, Inga Gibb, Pam Gillan, Graham Wiseman. After the Concert, he and Betty went on holiday to Fraser's home in Essex, and his health seemed to improve. Back in Elgin, within a few weeks, he suffered a heart attack. He died on 14 August.

Many of the young people who had played with him that night in July attended his funeral service.

The obituary in *The Northern Scot* of the 17 August 1974, is disappointingly flat and factual, but there is no doubt that memories of Willie are, today, in 2006, still bright and charismatic to all who knew him, including his many pupils, and to those who saw and heard him play.

A portrait of Willie Macpherson is a complex pattern of light and shade. The lights were sure and bright: he was a supremely talented musician in both the classical and traditional fields. He was cultivated, witty and suave, great company. He was a fine composer and an inspired - and inspiring - teacher and leader. However, stories of his drinking have entered local legend, and the shadows were dark places and sometimes caused pain and separation from those who were closest to him. Like many creative people, Willie was haunted. What he might have achieved in a perfect world, nobody knows. What he did achieve, despite his demons, was remarkable.

His achievement is fairly represented in these pages; in an Elgin Strathspey and Reel Society that continues to thrive; in those of his recordings that survive; in the memories of those who knew him and loved him and were inspired by him; and in the collection of tunes that follows.

The Elgin Collection

By Willie Macpherson

1. Brumley Brae (Reel)
2. Bow Brig (March)
3. Sheriffmill (Reel)
4. Pansport Reel (Reel)
5. Pitgaveny, also known as Newmill Brig (Strathspey)
6. The Coleburn (Slow Air)
7. Harry Glasgow (Hornpipe)
8. Harry Glasgow (Slow Air)
9. Effie Glasgow of Longmorn (Strathspey)
10. Effie Glasgow of Longmorn (Hornpipe)
11. Mr A F Macpherson's Reel, also known as A Fiddler's Reel (Reel)
12. Mrs Fraser Macpherson's Strathspey (Strathspey)
13. James Macpherson (Reel)
14. James Macpherson (Strathspey)
15. The Elgin Strathspey and Reel Players (March)
16. The Elgin Strathspey and Reel Players (Strathspey)
17. The Elgin Strathspey and Reel Players (Reel)
18. The Elgin Junior Strathspey and Reel Players (March)
19. Fogwatt Burns Supper (March)
20. Johnston's Mill (Reel)

The composition of these tunes took place fairly sporadically over the period from 1953 to 1974. The normal process of initial publication was a familiar one in traditional music circles: Willlie produced a composition in manuscript and passed it to friends who copied it by hand - or, later, photocopied it - and circulated it more widely. The tunes thus became known by being played, informally at first, until some of them came to be known in much wider circles than others. Two of the tunes can be with certainty ascribed to 1954, and those associated with the The Elgin Strathspey and Reel Society to the years 1970 to 1974, following the re-formation of the Society. The final date of composition of most of the others probably belongs to the years after Willie's return to Elgin in 1966.

The naming of the tunes follows traditional patterns. Though his heroes, Marshall and Skinner, often named tunes to flatter particular individuals and so gain a few extra shillings in sponsorship for the publication of their collections, we can assume that Willie's titles - unmotivated by commercial interest - reflect his fondness for particular local places and people and the personal memories associated with them.

1   Brumley Brae (Reel)

Forty years ago the Brumley Brae was a country track leading from the Bow Brig to the walks in the Oakwood. It was a favourite walk of courting couples. The implications of taking a girl up the Brumley Brae were clear enough. The Brumley Brae today is a broad suburban road leading from the west of Bishopmill to the countryside to the north of the town. The romantic associations are probably lost. For a number of years the tune was regarded by Country Dance bands as a fine "modern" alternative to traditional tunes in selections for a range of dances in reel mode. However, at Jennifer Wilson's suggestion, the tune was adopted as the "original" tune for the new dance *Swiss Lassie,* (created by Rosi Betsche - *Royal Scottish Country Dance Society Book No. 39*) and its playing has accordingly been restricted in the Country Dance world. It remains, however, immensely popular with Strathspey and Reel societies across the world, and this fine reel is probably Willie's best-known composition.

2   Bow Brig (March)

The Bow (pronounced "bough") Brig stands on the road that leads from near Dr Gray's Hospital, northwards, past Oldmills, to the edge of the Morriston estate at Brumley Brae. Completed in 1635, this was the first stone bridge over the Lossie. It withstood the Muckle Spate of 1829, and the bulk of the structure is original. The Bow Brig is now busy with suburban traffic but was, for many years, part of a regular Sunday afternoon walking circuit along the Lossie banks, past Morriston playing fields, the Marywell bridge and the long-gone Stepping Stones.

3   Sheriffmill (Reel)

Another picturesque spot on the Lossie. Sheriffmill, now a house, was one of the ancient mills of Elgin. It stands about half a mile upstream from the Bow Brig on the links of the Lossie to the west of the town. The Sheriffmill Brig was, until the late 1950s, the crossing point of the main road to Forres over the river.

4   Pansport (Reel)

Pansport is a historic and a picturesque site, close to the Cathedral and to the River Lossie. The precinct of Elgin Cathedral was enclosed within a stone wall, six and a half feet wide, about 12 feet high and 900 yards in circuit. Virtually all that remains of this enclosure is the Pansport, the east gate, that led to the meadows or "pans", and a 30 yard or so stretch of wall. The Macpherson family lived for a time in the 1930s at 10 Pansport Place, a pleasant sandstone square that encloses the splendid South College and a further stretch of the ancient precinct wall.

5 Pitgaveny, also known as Newmill Brig (Strathspey)

Pitgaveny is a small estate to the north of Elgin. It has been, tentatively, identified as the place where Macbeth won the battle as a result of which he gained the crown of Scotland. In the 1960s, a stone that, in legend, marked the spot where King Duncan died, was dug up, but nothing was found. In Willie's lifetime, Pitgaveny was the home of James Brander Dunbar, The Lairdie, John Buchan's inspiration for the poaching syndicate in *John MacNab*. Pitgaveny was also home to the kenspeckle figure of John Macdonald, The Singing Molecatcher, folk singer and composer (*The Rovin' Ploughboy*, *The Plooin' Match o' Duffus*, *Pitgaveny's Bonny Wuids*), melodeon player, diddler, puppeteer and general entertainer. The title of this tune may derive from Pitgaveny's popularity as a destination for Sunday morning walks for Willie and his granddaughter, Heather, and his dog Sheila. Newmill Brig is another name for the Brewery Brig, the picturesque old bridge near the Cathedral.

6 The Coleburn (Slow Air)

Coleburn Distillery, a former Scottish Malt Distillers' establishment, out of commission since the mid-1970s, stands about five miles south of Elgin just off the Rothes road. We are reliably informed that the inspiration for the title of

Willie's best-known Slow Air was not Coleburn's single malt - still available from Gordon & Macphail - but the very attractive grouping of larches, Scots pines and rhododendrons that flank the entrance of the steeply sloping drive down to the distillery.

7 Harry Glasgow (Hornpipe)
8 Harry Glasgow (Slow Air)
9 Effie Glasgow of Longmorn (Strathspey)
10 Effie Glasgow of Longmorn (Hornpipe)

Harry Glasgow came to work for the Customs and Excise Service in the Elgin area in 1961 when the Station in Plockton closed down. He was Exciseman at both Longmorn and Macallan Distilleries. He and Effie soon became involved in the musical and cultural world of Elgin. Effie, whose family had owned a hotel in Plockton, was a Mod Silver Medallist for singing, and Harry - an Englishman from Aylesbury - was an enthusiastic devotee of the traditional Scots fiddle. They became friends of Willie and supported his efforts to revive the Elgin Strathspey and Reel Society. The first recorded meeting of the new Society took place in the Exciseman's House at Longmorn in January 1970. Harry also made fiddles, one of which was played and complimented upon by Yehudi Menuhin. The Glasgows retired to Plockton in the early 1970s. Harry died in 1989 and Effie in 2000. They were always proud of their friendship with Willie and deeply conscious of the rare privilege of having their own tunes. The Slow

Strathspey and The Hornpipe, both entitled Effie Glasgow of Longmorn, were selected by Willie to play in the final of the BBC Scotland Scots Fiddle-playing Competition of 1969, which the Glasgows attended.

11   Mr A. F Macpherson's Reel, also known as A Fiddler's Reel.
12   Mrs Fraser Macpherson's Strathspey

These two tunes date from 1954. They were written in honour of Mr Alexander Fraser Macpherson WS (1896 - 1968), the Edinburgh solicitor who was first Honorary Treasurer and long-time Secretary of the Clan Macpherson Association, and his wife , Mrs Minnie Macpherson (nee Fraser). Mr Macpherson was a distinguished historian of Clan matters. The Macphersons were country dance enthusiasts. Willie had no connection with the Clan Association. It seems likely that he made the acquaintance of the Macphersons while playing at Country Dance occasions in the Edinburgh area in 1954, prior to his joining the SNO. Both tunes appeared on the record Dances of Scotland SR33102, issued by The Park Film Studios Players under the auspices of The Clan Macpherson to introduce two new Scottish Country Dances - Lady Stewart Macpherson's Reel and the Strathspey, The Macphersons of Edinburgh. The Strathspey printed here was played for the dance The Macphersons of Edinburgh, and the Reel was played by Willie in the Traditional Fiddling Interlude

on the record. The Park Film Studio Players comprised, in addition to Willie, James Burnett (guitar), James Robertson (bass) and Olive Ogston (piano). The Strathspey is regarded, both by fiddlers and by the Scottish Country Dance fraternity, as an especially beautiful tune.

13   James Macpherson (Reel)
14   James Macpherson (Strathspey)

The story of James "Neefie" Macpherson, father of seven, pattern weaver, self-taught musician, bandmaster has been told earlier. Sufficient to say here that he was the driving figure behind the early stages of his son's musical career. Willie composed these tunes some fifteen years after his father's death.

15   The Elgin Strathspey and Reel Players (March)
16   The Elgin Strathspey and Reel Players (Strathspey)
17   The Elgin Strathspey and Reel Players (Reel)
18   The Elgin Junior Strathspey and Reel Players (March)
19   Fogwatt Burns Supper (March)

The composition of these five tunes can be assigned to the period from 1970 - the date of the revival of the Elgin Strathspey and Reel Society - to 1974. Fogwatt is a hamlet about four miles to the south of Elgin on the Rothes road. The Burns Supper of 1970 held in the Fogwatt Hall was one of the first public engagements of the re-formed Society. Willie composed this march to mark the occasion. It has been played at the annual Burns Supper in Fogwatt ever since.

20   Johnston's Mill (Reel)

Johnstons of Elgin is one Scotland's best-known textile manufacturing companies. Established in 1800, the company became famous for its "estate tweeds" but soon diversified into softer fabrics and pioneered the manufacture of garments in cashmere and vicuna. Today it has a world-wide reputation for the excellence of its products, and its millshop, the Cashmere Centre, attracts touristsfrom all over the world. Willie's father, James Macpherson, worked all his life at Johnston's Mill, and the Johnston family played important roles in the musical education of both Willie and Ernest.

Two Tunes in Tribute to Willie Macpherson

1   William Macpherson (Slow Hornpipe)

The Shetland Fiddler Arthur Scott Robertson beat Willie into 2nd place in the Scottish National Fiddle Competition, sponsored by the BBC, in 1969. Born in Bressay in 1911, he became a fiddler/violinist of the highest calibre and a profilic composer of traditional tunes. His collection of Musical Reflections runs to five volumes. Among his best-known tunes are *Bert Murray - Man of Music*, *Memories of Hector MacAndrew*, *That Elegant Style and Strathspey Forever*. This Slow Hornpipe, was composed in 1990 with the tribute: "to William Macpherson, Elgin, gifted violinist and fiddler".

2   Willie Macpherson's Polka (Polka)

Born in Fyvie but brought up in the Elgin area - and another pupil of Kim Murray - Bill Brian knew Willie as well as anyone did in the last years of his life. Returning to Elgin from Aberdeen in 1969, Bill soon became involved with Willie in reviving the Elgin Strathspey and Reel Society. With Willie as Conductor and Bill as Leader, the Society went from strength to strength. Following Willie's death in 1974, Bill took over as Conductor and led the Society to victories in all the major festivals and at the National Mod in 1977. He continues, in 2005, to conduct the Society. In 1978, he won the supreme solo award in traditional fiddle playing when he became Golden Fiddle champion. He composed Willie Macpherson's Polka on Willie's death in 1974. The tune won the Composers' Competition at the Elgin Strathspey and Reel Society's Festival in 1975. The judge, BBC producer, John Crawford, declared that the tune "in its jauntiness, typified the essence of Willie's nature".

Brumley Brae

Reel

William Macpherson

Bow Brig

March

William Macpherson

Variation

Fine

D.C. al fine

Sheriffmill

Reel

William Macpherson

Pansport Reel

Reel

William Macpherson

Pitgaveny, also known as Newmill Brig (Strathspey)

Strathspey

William Macpherson

The Coleburn

Slow Air

William Macpherson

Harry Glasgow's Hornpipe

Hornpipe

William Macpherson

Harry Glasgow

Slow Air in Strathspey style

William Macpherson

LONGMORN
DISTILLERY

DUTY FREE
WAREHOUSE
No 17/18

Effie Glasgow of Longmorn

Strathspey

William Macpherson

Effie Glasgow's Hornpipe

Hornpipe

William Macpherson

Mr A. F. Macpherson's Reel
(Also known as 'A Fiddler's Reel')

Reel

William Macpherson

Mrs. Fraser Macpherson's Strathspey

William Macpherson

Strathspey

James Macpherson's Reel

Reel

William Macpherson

James Macpherson's Strathspey

Strathspey

William Macpherson

Elgin Strathspey & Reel Players

March

William Macpherson

Elgin Strathspey & Reel Players

Strathspey

William Macpherson

Elgin Strathspey & Reel Players

Reel

William Macpherson

The Elgin Junior Strathspey & Reel Players

March

William Macpherson

The Fogwatt Burns Supper

March

William Macpherson

Johnston's Mill

Reel

William Macpherson

William Macpherson

Arthur Scott Robinson

Slow Hornpipe

Willie Macpherson's Polka

Polka

Bill Brian

Photographic Notes and Credits

The majority of photographs used in the book come from the Macpherson family collection or have been specially taken by the book's designer, Graeme Nairn. Notes have not been provided in cases where the subject of a photograph is self-explanatory. In some cases, it has proved impossible to ascribe names to all the individuals who appear in a group photograph.

p11   Detail of portrait of William Marshall, by John Moir, in Scottish National Portrait Gallery.

p13   Scott Skinner

p15   Macpherson family in 1927. Back from left: Effie, Sophia, Meggie, James; front: Ethel, Ernest, Dickie, Aunt, Willie.

p16   (i) Family on shore at Cummingston in 1937. From left: Willie, Meggie, Ethel, Jackie Macpherson, Sophia, Adela, James.

         (ii) Sophia and James 1955.

p17   (i) BBC Theatre Orchestra, 1932. Ernest is seated 4th from left.

         (ii) Meggie and Ethel.

p18   P J Proby with touring ensemble in 1964. Dickie is on the front right of the photograph with the baton.

p22   The Reel and Strathspey Band of Boys, 1939. Back from left: Jim Hutcheson, Jock Clayton, Alan McKenzie, Willie, Alan Shearer, ?, Hamish Anderson, Jimmy Taylor; front: ?, George Grassick, Ian McHardy, Donald McHardy, George MacDonald, Robin Stuart

p23   (i) Willie in the RAF. In the group photograph, he is second from the left of the front row.

         (ii) Betty and Willie on their wedding day, 1939.

p24   (i) Family on holiday in Edinburgh, 1955. Back from left: Fraser, Willie, Betty; front: Ian, Elizabeth

         (ii) A local "pickup" band, 1949. From left: Willie, Johnnie Thompson, Pat Fraser, Meggie.

p26   Annie Shand Scott Band, 1955.

p27   Willie providing light relief during rehearsal.

p28   Willie teaches Yehudi Menuhin how to play the fiddle, 1962.

p30   SNO in Concert, Royal Festival hall, 1956.

p32   Photo courtesy of The Scotsman Publications. Photographer: Robert Perry

p36   (i) The earliest photograph of the revived Elgin Strathspey and Reel Society. Standing from left: Harry Glasgow, Bill Brian, Willie, George Welsh, George Bremner; front: Inga Gibb, Lizzie Geddes.

p37   (ii) The Elgin Junior Strathspey and Reel Players, 1972. Back from left: Eileen Geddes, Elizabeth Hanley, Roderick Cromar, Eoin Grassick, Kenneth Lyndsay, Stuart Huyton, Maureen McMurran; front: ?, Moira Wilson; Shirley Potts, Sarah Laurenson; Keith Collins.

         (iii) Willie rehearsing in Elgin Academy with the Saturday Morning Schools' Orchestra.

         (iv) Willie with pupils at the summer school in Grantown in 1972.

p46   Photo courtesy of Moray Local Heritage Service.

p50   Photo courtesy of Moray Local Heritage Service.

p82   Alexander Nasmyth   Robert Burns   Scottish National Portrait Gallery

Richard Bennett

Born and brought up in the Elgin area,
Richard Bennett has taught English in Dundee,
Fochabers and Elgin. He retired in 2002.

Bill Brian

Bill Brian, founder member, leader and conductor
of the revived Elgin Strathspey and Reel Society,
is one of Scotland's most respected fiddlers.
Brought up in the Elgin area, Bill worked for the
Hydro Board. Now retired, he devotes all his time
to playing, conducting, teaching and
composing for the Scots fiddle.

Graeme Nairn

Born in Montrose, Graeme Nairn, after studying at
Duncan of Jordanstone College of Art, Dundee, has
worked as a freelance designer and for the last
twenty-five years as designer at Moray College, Elgin.